The Bill of Rights

The RIGHT to PRIVACY in the HOME

THE THIRD AMENDMENT

John Rokutani

Enslow Publishing
101 W. 23rd Street
Suite 240
New York, NY 10011
USA

enslow.com

Published in 2018 by Enslow Publishing, LLC.
101 W. 23rd Street, Suite 240, New York, NY 10011

Library of Congress Cataloging-in-Publication Data

Names: Rokutani, John, author.
   Title: The right to privacy in the home : the Third Amendment / John Rokutani.
   Description: New York, NY : Enslow Publishing, 2018. | Series: The bill of rights |
      Audience: Grades 5-8 | Includes bibliographical references and index.
   Identifiers: LCCN 2017003053| ISBN 9780766085534 (library-bound) | ISBN
      9780766087316 (pbk.) | ISBN 9780766087323 (6-pack)
   Subjects: LCSH: United States. Constitution. 3rd Amendment—Juvenile literature.
      | Requisitions, Military—United States—History—Juvenile literature.
   Classification: LCC KF4558 3rd .R65 2018 | DDC 342.7308/58—dc23
   LC record available at https://lccn.loc.gov/2017003053

Printed in China

To Our Readers: We have done our best to make sure all website addresses in this book were active and appropriate when we went to press. However, the author and the publisher have no control over and assume no liability for the material available on those websites or on any websites they may link to. Any comments or suggestions can be sent by e-mail to customerservice@enslow.com.

Photo Credits: Cover, p. 1 Africa Studio/Shutterstock.com; cover, interior pages (background) A-R-T/Shutterstock.com; cover, interior pages (quill) Leporska Lyubov/ Shutterstock.com; p. 4 © North Wind Picture Archives; pp. 9, 13 MPI/Archive Photos/ Getty Images; p. 17 GraphicaArtis/Archive Photos/Getty Images; p. 19 Francis G. Mayer/Corbis/Getty Images; p. 22 Michael Ventura/Alamy Stock Photo; p. 25 Library of Congress; p. 29 Stephen Morton/Getty Images; p. 30 Corbis/Getty Images; p. 34 John Moore/Getty Images; p. 36 Tinnaporn Sathapornnanont/Shutterstock.com; p. 38 Bettmann/Getty Images; p. 40 Stephen J. Boitano/LightRocket/Getty Images; p. 41 © AP Images.

Contents

British soldiers, identifiable by their uniforms' red coats, demand to be "quartered" in an American colonist's home. To be quartered somewhere is to be allowed to stay there.

INTRODUCTION

There was a time in American colonial history when the British government forced colonists to open their homes to British soldiers. British soldiers could move in, demanding comfortable lodging and food. They could easily steal from or vandalize the colonists' houses. This practice of housing soldiers was known as quartering, and it was one of the major causes of the American Revolution.

After the Revolution, Americans wanted to prevent similar abuses by their new government. This was so important to the framers of the Constitution that they formally outlawed the practice of quartering in the Third Amendment. The amendment reads:

> **No soldier shall, in time of peace be quartered in any house, without the consent of the owner, nor in time of war, but in manner to be prescribed by law.**

Over the years, the Third Amendment has been the subject of very little controversy, especially when compared to the other amendments of the Bill of Rights. The housing of soldiers during times of war hasn't even been a question since the 1860s during the Civil War. However, the amendment, in combination with others, is the basis of the constitutional right to privacy.

CHAPTER ONE

THE INTOLERABLE ACT *of* QUARTERING

For about 150 years, the American colonists lived in relative peace under British rule. The colonists were far from Great Britain, but they remained loyal to the British government. In the 1760s, however, the British government began to exercise greater control over the colonies, and things started to change.

THE COLONIES AND GREAT BRITAIN

By the mid-eighteenth century, relations between the American colonists and their rulers in Great Britain had become strained. The colonists saw themselves as key to the expansion of the British Empire. Away from the eastern coastal areas, North America was largely unexplored and sparsely settled by European colonists. The colonists viewed the Native Americans who had lived on the continent for thousands of years with fear and suspicion. The vast land west of the Appalachian Mountains was virtually unknown to the settlers.

The colonists had some measure of self-government. Colonial charters gave the thirteen colonies the right to maintain their own government assemblies, though decisions by these assemblies were understood to remain under control of the British Parliament. The colonial assemblies had authority only over their own affairs, and any legislation passed by an assembly had to be approved in England by the country's Board of Trade before it could go into effect. The colonies were seen as a business venture, and the Board of Trade denied them the right to oversee matters relating to trade. The assemblies operated much the same way as Parliament. Only free men who owned property had the right to vote or hold office. Women, slaves, and indentured servants could not vote. However, the sheer size of the colonies allowed a much larger number of colonists to be property owners than in England, giving a larger portion of the population a voice in the political process.

Another factor that contributed to the growing sense of independence held by the colonists was the English government's neglect of the colonies. The colonies were mostly undeveloped and, compared to England, insignificant in terms of their population and economy. Beginning in the mid-1600s, the English government became preoccupied with its own affairs. These included the English Civil War (1641–1651) and a series of wars against France that were fought both in Europe and in the colonies with the help of of the colonists. In the midst of this turmoil, the colonies were largely given free rein to oversee their affairs. Colonial governments made laws, regulated their own courts and militias, established new counties, and raised revenue to pay the costs of government with little oversight from England.

This pattern continued for about 120 years, until the end of the French and Indian War (1754–1763), which forced France to give up its claim to land east of the Mississippi River. The war was very expensive for the British, who wanted the colonists to help pay the expense in return for preventing a French takeover of the colonies. At this time, the British also realized the growing importance of raw materials, such as timber and iron ore, which were imported from America. Great Britain began moving to tighten its hold on the colonies.

The colonists, however, resisted these efforts. They felt that they had already contributed to the war effort by providing supplies and troops for the colonial militias, which fought beside British troops. They also did not believe that they had profited from the outcome of the war.

TAXATION WITHOUT REPRESENTATION

Soon after the war ended, the British government began imposing new restrictions on the colonists. Parliament's Proclamation Act of 1763 forbade colonists from settling west of the Appalachian Mountains. The act angered colonists, who believed they had risked their lives to drive the French from

The leader of Britain's forces during the French and Indian War was Edward Braddock, seen here leading his soldiers toward Fort Duquesne in Pennsylvania.

the region. Another law, the Sugar Act of 1764, enforced the collection of a tax on molasses brought into the colonies from the Caribbean. The colonists felt that the tax was imposed unjustly without their consent.

Anger in the colonies continued to grow as Great Britain exercised its right to impose taxes and regulations on the colonists. In 1765, Parliament passed the Stamp Act and the Mutiny Act. The Stamp Act required that all documents, such as newspapers, wills, and court orders, carry a special stamp. The stamps could only be bought with silver coins, rather than with the paper money and barter system that many colonists used.

The colonists were furious about the Stamp Act, though a similar act had been in place in England for centuries and the stamps sold in the colonies were cheaper than those sold in England. Colonists referred to the Stamp Act and the earlier taxes as "taxation without representation." They felt it was unfair that they should be taxed by Parliament without having a member of Parliament representing their interests. Colonists protested loudly about the act, sometimes forming angry mobs and attacking tax collectors.

The British government had not anticipated such a reaction and moved to lift the tax in 1766. However, other taxes and laws passed during the 1760s remained in place and continued to anger colonists.

THE QUARTERING ACT

Of the acts that remained in place, none had a greater impact than the Quartering Act, also known as the Mutiny Act. The Quartering Act required that the colonial assemblies set aside money to house the British troops stationed in the colonies and provide them with food and supplies. Ordinarily, British soldiers in the colonies were housed in buildings called barracks, where dozens of soldiers could live at one time. However, if there were more soldiers stationed in a town than there were barracks, they were to be moved into such buildings as inns, barns, and empty houses.

The law was passed by Parliament as a means to ensure that the colonies paid for their own military protection. Colonial leaders, however, argued that they provided their own defense through militias made up of armed colonists. They resented having to pay to house soldiers whom they felt were not needed. They also felt that the act violated English laws dating back to 1111, when the London city charter forbade the quartering of soldiers within the city walls. The English Bill of Rights of 1689 also made quartering illegal, though the law's reach was never extended to any of the British colonies.

Colonists also interpreted the Quartering Act as a way to control them by presenting a show of force. At the time, the British government kept a standing army of ten thousand soldiers in the colonies. Other laws passed around the same time gave the British greater power to conduct trials without juries and to limit the freedom of the press. Protests continued throughout the colonies, and anti-British sentiment grew.

THE SEEDS OF REBELLION

Tensions between the colonists and British soldiers stationed in Boston boiled over on March 5, 1770. An angry mob formed at the city's Custom House after a guard attacked a group of boys who had been taunting him. The mob grew to an estimated three hundred to four hundred people. The soldiers who responded to the incident eventually opened fire on the crowd, hitting eleven men. Three were killed at the scene, and another two later died of their wounds. This incident would become known as the Boston Massacre.

The Boston Massacre was used as a rallying point by colonial figures such as Samuel Adams and Paul Revere to fuel rebellious sentiment. All but two of the soldiers accused of firing the shots were tried and acquitted. Colonists who had been indifferent to the British presence saw the violent incident as an unnecessary show of force in the city's streets. If the Quartering Act had not been passed, the British soldiers would have been garrisoned outside of the city.

Later incidents of colonial unrest in Massachusetts would lead the British to pass stronger laws. The most famous of these events is the Boston Tea Party. In 1773, Parliament's passage of the Tea Act made the East India Company the only company that could sell tea in the colonies. The colonists would pay less for their tea, though the price would include a small duty, or tax. The colonists protested strongly against the tax. In New York City and Philadelphia, they refused to unload the ships carrying the tea. In Boston, colonists famously boarded tea ships at night and threw the tea into the harbor.

INTOLERABLE ACTS

The British passed a second quartering act aimed at quieting the protests in Massachusetts. The Quartering Act of 1774

The Boston Tea Party took place on December 16, 1773. A number of Boston-based rebels disguised as Native Americans snuck onto merchant ships and threw tea into Boston Harbor to protest the Tea Act, passed in May of that year.

expanded the earlier Quartering Act. Like the first law, it stated that soldiers who demanded shelter be provided with suitable quarters within twenty-four hours. If suitable barracks were not provided for soldiers, the soldiers were to be put up in empty houses, outbuildings, and inns. The act went further than the previous law. It stated that the owners of the properties were directly responsible for making sure that the soldiers were fed and supplied with clothing, equipment, and other necessities.

Along with the other laws, the Quartering Act was labeled one of the "Intolerable Acts" by the colonists. In 1774, delegates from each of the colonies except Georgia met in Philadelphia to discuss a response to the laws. Acting together, the delegates to this First Continental Congress decided to boycott British imports and send a list of resolutions called the Declaration of Rights and Grievances to Great Britain. Parliament rejected the declaration, and on April 19, 1775, the Revolutionary War broke out between

AMERICA'S FIRST FEDERAL GOVERNMENT

Before the Constitution, the United States' federal government was laid out in a document called the Articles of Confederation. The Articles of Confederation set up a weak central government. They allowed the Continental Congress to conduct international diplomacy, to print money, and to raise a military.

The states were so powerful under the articles that they were able to behave as individual nations. States could leave the confederation at any time. And with no greater oversight, states started to pass laws in direct conflict with other states. The framers saw a need for a much stronger federal government and created it in the Constitution.

The Bill of Rights

the British and the colonists in Massachusetts at the Battles of Lexington and Concord.

The delegates met again that May as the Second Continental Congress and decided to take steps toward independence. They raised an army, established trade regulations, sent ambassadors to other nations, and encouraged the colonies to set up local governments. In 1776, the delegates ratified the Declaration of Independence, a document that set forth the reasons for breaking free from Great Britain, including their objection to quartering troops. The delegates also began working on a document called the Articles of Confederation and Perpetual Union that would serve as a forerunner to the US Constitution. Ratified in 1781, the articles formally created the United States of America.

CHAPTER TWO

THE FRAMERS
and the
THIRD AMENDMENT

The Articles of Confederation created a loose union of states and a weak central federal government. However, the articles left openings for conflict among the states, especially as they passed contradictory laws and vied for control of the West.

In 1787, delegates from twelve states (Rhode Island was not represented) met in Philadelphia for a national conference established by the Continental Congress. The delegates were given the task of strengthening and improving the Articles of Confederation. In all, fifty-five delegates attended the convention, including leaders such as George Washington, Thomas Jefferson, and Benjamin Franklin.

This painting of the signing of the Constitution in 1787 now hangs in the United States Capitol building. Among the delegates pictured are Thomas Jefferson, Benjamin Franklin, and George Washington.

THE CONSTITUTION

The Constitutional Convention met from May 25 to September 17, 1787. While the original purpose of the convention was simply to consider amending the Articles of Confederation, it ultimately resulted in radical changes to the government. The delegates themselves represented a broad range of opinions about the nation's future. They wanted what they believed to be the best outcome for their states on matters such as representation in Congress. Debate went on for days—and sometimes weeks—on matters such as whether or not to forbid slavery.

One of the most influential delegates was James Madison of Virginia. Madison had studied governments around the world and believed that the United States needed a strong central government. He wrote a series of fifteen resolutions called the Virginia Plan that proposed drastic changes to the government. The Virginia Plan proposed that the federal government have the power to make laws and enforce them through the executive and judicial branches. It also proposed the establishment of a bicameral Congress. While the states would retain many of their powers, they would also be part of a national government. Madison's Virginia Plan would ultimately form the basis of the federal government.

The document was finally completed and signed on September 17, 1787. However, the work of the delegates had not ended. They had to return to their states and have the new document ratified, or approved, before it could become law. When nine of the thirteen states ratified the document, the Constitution would be considered accepted and a new government would be formed.

However, the delegates had their work cut out for them. The colonial conventions disagreed about the proposed national government. One faction, called the Federalists, believed in the concept of a strong central government. The Anti-Federalists wanted the states to remain in control of their own destiny while staying loosely united. The Federalists ultimately won the debate by presenting a formal plan of government, by gaining the support of land-owning men who could vote, and through the persuasive arguments of famous Federalists such as Benjamin Franklin, Alexander Hamilton, James Madison, and George Washington.

By July 1788, all of the states had ratified the Constitution except North Carolina and Rhode Island. These two states waited until after the inauguration of George

Alexander Hamilton was the very first secretary of the treasury. His face appears on the ten dollar bill.

Washington as the first president of the United States in 1789. However, even after the US Constitution had been ratified by all thirteen states, some leaders continued to criticize the document for not doing enough to protect individual freedoms.

THE FIRST TEN AMENDMENTS

Some of the Founding Fathers decided that they needed to win over the most prominent critics of the Constitution, otherwise the young nation ran the risk of breaking apart.

DEFENDING THE CONSTITUTION

During the process of ratifying the Constitution, Alexander Hamilton and other Federalists worried that the document would be rejected because it called for a strong central government. Hamilton felt that he needed to create strong public support for the document to guarantee its ratification. Hamilton, James Madison, and John Jay wrote a series of eighty-five articles that attempted to explain the strengths of the Constitution and why the document was needed. The essays were printed in several newspapers between October 1787 and August 1788. The authors wished to keep their identities secret and published the essays under the pseudonym Publicus.

The essays were used in the debate over ratification in New York and Virginia. Today, they are considered among the most important writings about the Constitution and are still used by the Supreme Court to determine the intentions of the Founding Fathers. The fact that the essays argued against passage of a Bill of Rights shows that a lively debate continued over the need for such a document.

The Bill of Rights

These critics (among them Thomas Jefferson) thought that the Constitution should guarantee specific rights. They wanted a Bill of Rights to protect citizens and ensure that the nation's government would never become tyrannical, as they felt Great Britain's had in the years leading up to the Revolutionary War.

However, others objected to the idea of a Bill of Rights. They worried that by attaching a list of rights to the Constitution, they would limit protection only to those rights. However, similar bills had already been passed. In fact, the colonists had lived under such a bill until the Revolutionary War. In 1689, Parliament passed the English Bill of Rights to protect the basic freedoms of English subjects.

As the thirteen colonies began breaking away from Great Britain in 1776, George Mason referred to the English Bill of Rights when drafting the Virginia Bill of Rights. The Virginia Bill of Rights outlined the right to life, liberty, and property and described government as being the servant of the people. Mason's document influenced Thomas Jefferson as he wrote the Declaration of Independence and influenced the creation of the Bill of Rights. Mason was among the delegates to the Constitutional Convention who did not sign the document because it did not include a Bill of Rights. James Madison took up the work of creating the Bill of Rights. He began by taking suggestions from other Founding Fathers who felt that individual freedoms needed to be protected. Madison condensed these suggestions and presented them to Congress as a Bill of Rights amending the Constitution on June 8, 1789. Congress approved twelve of the amendments and sent them out to the states to be ratified. All thirteen states ratified ten of the amendments, and they went into effect in 1791 as the Bill of Rights.

The Bill of Rights is one of the most famous documents in the nation's history. Many of the amendments in the bill were written as a direct response to the pre–Revolutionary War laws passed by the British. The Founding Fathers wanted to guarantee that citizens would not have to live

You can see an original copy of the Bill of Rights at the rotunda of the Washington, DC, National Archives.

through a similar loss of liberties. Amendments that specifically protected basic freedoms included the First Amendment, which guarantees freedom of speech, press, religion, assembly, and petition; the Second Amendment, which guarantees the right to bear arms; and the Fourth Amendment, which prohibits unreasonable searches and seizures of property. The Bill of Rights states that people have rights not specifically listed and that the federal government derives its power solely from the Constitution.

OUTLAWING THE INTOLERABLE

Like the Fourth Amendment, the Third Amendment was drafted as a direct response to the Quartering Act. This act proved to be a major burden to colonists before the Revolutionary War. The presence of the soldiers in towns and on private property was supposed to make the colonists less likely to rise up against the government. British officials reasoned that by quartering soldiers with known troublemakers, they could possibly put an end to the civil unrest that was threatening their control of the colonies. They also believed that since the British army had fought to defend the colonies from the French during the French and Indian War, the colonists should provide some portion of the army's upkeep while troops were stationed there.

Many colonists had remained deeply loyal to the British government, and many colonial leaders wanted to make peace with the British. However, the British had greatly miscalculated the colonists' feelings about British soldiers living in their midst. This was particularly true in the Massachusetts colony and in the city of Boston, where anti-British sentiment ran high.

During the Revolutionary War, both British and American soldiers were quartered with private citizens. Soldiers from George Washington's Continental army were quartered in private homes by the New York Provincial Congress. However, Washington and other American military leaders opposed the practice of quartering. They largely avoided the situation by staying away from towns, using public buildings, and building their own barracks. As a result, American troops were seldom quartered with private citizens. The relatively few instances of quartering occurred early in the war, before the states had a chance to make provisions for housing soldiers.

By the time the war ended, the governments of Delaware, Massachusetts, and Maryland had passed laws to protect citizens from having to quarter troops during peacetime. The laws did allow for quartering troops in times of war, but only under the direction of the state legislatures.

DRAFTING THE THIRD AMENDMENT

James Madison himself introduced the Third Amendment after repeatedly hearing concerns that soldiers could be quartered in private homes. The British Quartering Act was still

General George Washington appears here before the Battle of Yorktown, which ended in a decisive victory for the American colonists in 1781. To the left is the Marquis de Lafayette, and on the right, riding out of the frame, is Alexander Hamilton.

very fresh in the minds of citizens and lawmakers, though the US Army consisted largely of local militias at the time.

Some leaders felt that it was absolutely necessary to maintain a regular, well-trained standing army. They knew that the threat from other nations was too great to rely on private citizens who may or may not have been able to perform their militia duties if needed. Though he publicly praised militias, George Washington himself wrote privately to other leaders and urged them to support maintaining a standing army.

Ultimately, it was decided that during times of peace, soldiers would be garrisoned in forts and camps close to towns and cities (and even within their borders), but that their quarters would be kept entirely separate from private property. Soldiers could also seek lodgings on their own, but they would not be able to demand them as British soldiers had done and would have to pay their own expenses. The language of the amendment specifically states that soldiers cannot demand shelter from private citizens in peacetime.

The wording of the amendment leaves open the possibility of quartering during wartime. Madison and other Founding Fathers recognized that the young nation might have to fight again for its independence. While the British had left forts and garrison buildings throughout their former colonies, there could be no guarantee that any fighting that might occur would take place near such structures. In such cases, soldiers might have needed to use private homes or buildings for officer headquarters, for storage, or even as hospitals.

CHAPTER THREE

THE THIRD AMENDMENT *in* AMERICAN HISTORY

Perhaps the most straightforward amendment of the Bill of Rights, the Third Amendment is narrow in focus and has been the subject of very little controversy over the years. The Supreme Court has heard only one case directly addressing the Third Amendment. The quartering of troops during war hasn't been a question since the nineteenth century, during the Civil War. Even though the amendment isn't often in the news or cited in court cases, it does guarantee that the United States will house its military.

SOLDIERS' QUARTERS

The Third Amendment requires that, to stay in a home during peacetime, a soldier must have the consent of the property owner. Soldiers and other military personnel who rent or lease their quarters from a landlord are bound by the same legal obligations as other tenants. It is understood that they occupy their dwelling with the consent of their landlord, who maintains the right to evict them if just cause is found, as with any other tenant.

Many full-time military service members today live in quarters located on military bases, though some service members are allowed to live off base. These arrangements free the military from worrying about possible Third Amendment violations. Other military personnel may live rent-free with their family members, again provided they have the consent of the property owner or own their own homes.

For personnel in the National Guard or reserve forces who are not full-time members of the service, a clear distinction is made between when they are on active duty and when they are not. When on active duty, these service members are housed on military bases. At other times, they are left to make their own housing arrangements.

QUARTERING AND WAR

During a time of war, soldiers can be quartered in private homes, though such a case has not occurred since the nineteenth century. According to the Bill of Rights, when quartering is allowed, it is supposed to be regulated under rules set forth by Congress. During the War of 1812 (1812–1815), the United States had formally declared war against

Military housing at Fort Stewart, Georgia, in 2008. At the time of this photo, these barracks had just been built.

Great Britain. Congress failed to set forth any regulations for the act of quartering, but soldiers were quartered in private homes at the time.

Quartering was widespread during the Civil War, when hundreds of thousands of Union soldiers marched into the South to force the Confederacy to rejoin the United States. Both armies constantly took advantage of private property during the war. They camped and fought on farmers' fields, fed themselves on crops and livestock, and commandeered private houses and other buildings for their own use.

The Union army faced unique circumstances during the Civil War. The federal government had not recognized

This image shows a federal hospital meant for the use of the Union army in Fair Oaks, Virginia. Armies often had to use houses as makeshift hospitals in the Civil War.

the South's right to secede from the Union. This meant that the eleven states making up the Confederacy were still—in the eyes of Congress—part of the United States. However, the Confederacy now saw itself as an independent entity. The Confederate states had set up their own government, raised an army, and printed currency. They had control of forts and other federal facilities located in the South. They considered the Union army to be an invading force. President Abraham Lincoln and Congress were faced with the unpleasant choice of either disregarding the Third Amendment—and a number of other constitutional rights— or allowing the South to break away. Northern soldiers were even quartered on private lands in states that had remained loyal to the Union.

Quartering was widespread in the North, and the army seized the homes of loyal citizens to use as barracks. This practice was so common that the military even created a system for handling rent claims resulting from the seizure and use of homes by the military. Ultimately, about $500,000 in claims for rent and damage to property came in from property owners in Union states, and another $2.5 million came in from homeowners in Confederate states. There was some question as to whether the quartering of soldiers on the property of loyal citizens was a violation of the Third Amendment. Technically, Congress never declared war on the Confederacy and saw the Civil War as an act of putting down an insurrection, rather than a full-on military conquest. Though the act of secession by the South created a state of war, Congress never acted to regulate quartering on Union territory. Instead, it was left to the executive branch—President Abraham Lincoln and his cabinet—to judge that the state of civil unrest was so great and the threat that it posed to the nation was serious enough to permit the act of quartering.

THE CASE OF *ENGBLOM v. CAREY*

In 1982, the Second Circuit US Court of Appeals heard the case of *Engblom v. Carey*. The case is the only lawsuit involving the quartering of soldiers to ever make it to a federal court of appeals. The case involved a 1979 strike by prison guards in New York. Governor Hugh Carey called in the National Guard to replace the guards who had left their jobs. The government ordered guards who lived at the prison in housing provided by the state to clear out of the houses to give the soldiers a place to stay.

Two of the guards sued the state, claiming that their Third Amendment rights had been violated because their homes had been occupied by soldiers against their wishes. The case was heard first by a district court, which threw it out because the guards did not own their homes at the prison. The appeals court ruled that the amendment applies to tenants and, that under the amendment, National Guard personnel are considered soldiers. It sent the case back to the district court, where it was rejected on a legal technicality—that the guards failed to show that the state knew that it was violating their rights.

The Bill of Rights

THE IMPACT OF THE THIRD AMENDMENT

The Third Amendment may not be well known to many people today, but it continues to have an effect on how the government reacts to domestic emergencies. It also has had an impact on how the government houses its troops. The military has maintained forts, large military encampments, and bases throughout the nation since the Revolutionary War. During the early years of the United States, the government was anxious to keep its soldiers out of the way of private citizens. During the eighteenth and nineteenth centuries, military forts and outposts located on the nation's frontier provided protection to civilians who faced real threats from attacking Native Americans and from the blizzards, wildfires, and other dangerous conditions that sometimes arose far from towns. When large numbers of settlers began moving west across the Great Plains, the US Army established forts near major trails to protect them. Most of the vast, empty prairie was considered government land, meaning that the military did not have to worry about coming into conflict with private citizens over property rights before establishing forts.

Settlers who ran into trouble could seek help at the nearest fort. Towns usually grew up near these forts and, in calmer parts of the country, around camps and bases. Even during the mid-twentieth century, a new military base could create a great deal of employment for a region. People would move into the area to work on the base or set up businesses that served the base workers and military personnel.

The American military expanded a base formerly belonging to the Soviet Army in Afghanistan. On the right is older, stone, Soviet-built housing and on the left is wooden, American-built housing.

Today, many private citizens earn their living by working on or around military bases. They run businesses such as shops and restaurants that cater to soldiers, or they work on the base as civilians. Military bases continue to serve as a major source of employment for some towns and cities. When the Defense Department threatens to close military bases because of budget cuts or for other reasons, nearby residents often protest the closures. They recognize that the bases play an important role in their lives, both economically and by giving their communities a sense of identity.

CHAPTER FOUR

THE CONSTITUTIONAL RIGHT *to* PRIVACY

Over time, the Third Amendment has come to be called the Bill of Rights' "forgotten amendment." Few Americans even think of quartering as something that might happen. The United States maintains a large standing army, which it houses on military bases across the country that are connected by the public interstate highway system.

Though it isn't as frequently cited in court cases as other amendments included in the Bill of Rights, the Third Amendment continues to work as intended and with little fuss. The fact that so few court cases have ever been heard regarding the Third Amendment serves as a testament to the clarity of its intentions. This may also serve as a reminder of the amendment's obscurity. During the Civil War, for example, no court challenges were made on constitutional grounds against the government for quartering soldiers. It is possible that many citizens were unaware of the amendment and the protection it provided.

THE SUPREME COURT AND THIRD AMENDMENT RIGHTS

Today, the Third Amendment is among the least-cited amendments to the Constitution. Since the Civil War, there

The United States Supreme Court building is located in Washington, DC, to the east of the Capitol builidng.

CONSTITUTIONAL AMENDMENTS

The framers wanted the Constitution to be able to adapt with changing times, so they built into it a process by which it could be changed, or amended. They made this process difficult enough that amendments couldn't be passed lightly, but not so difficult that amendments could never pass.

In order for an amendment to pass, it must first be proposed. An amendment can be proposed by either two-thirds of the state legislatures or by a two-thirds vote of both the Senate and the House of Representatives. Once proposed, three-fourths of the states must approve the amendment for it to become part of the Constitution. The Constitution has been amended twenty-seven times since it was ratified.

The Bill of Rights

have been no widespread instances of quartering in private homes. Unlike other amendments, it has seldom come up before the Supreme Court. The handful of court decisions that have drawn on the amendment have mostly dealt with matters far removed from quartering troops.

In 1965, the Supreme Court ruled in the case of *Griswold v. Connecticut*. The court's ruling found that a Connecticut law making it illegal for married couples to use birth control was unconstitutional because it violated the right to privacy in the home. The justices agreed that the Constitution does not specifically refer to a right to privacy, but that the right

These nine men made up the Supreme Court from 1962 to 1965. The chief justice at the time was Earl Warren, seen seated in the center.

to privacy is suggested by the Third Amendment and several other amendments.

The right to privacy was revisited in 1972, when the Supreme Court heard the case of *Eisenstadt v. Baird*. The case involved a birth control law similar to the one in Connecticut, except it applied to unmarried couples. The court ruled to uphold the right to privacy and that all birth control matters should remain private. Both cases played a role in the landmark 1973 *Roe v. Wade* case that made abortion legal in all fifty states.

PRIVACY IN THE HOME

The Third Amendment explicitly prohibits military personnel from demanding shelter in private homes during times of peace. It was written to prevent the military from exercising its power over citizens and to guarantee that it remained subordinate to civilian law, particularly within private homes. In the handful of Supreme Court rulings that have invoked the Third Amendment, it has also cast its protection against government intrusion in the home violating an unstated constitutional right to privacy. In the case *Griswold v. Connecticut*, the amendment was cited in the court's decision that some laws violated the Constitution by intruding into the private lives of citizens. The Founding Fathers wanted to draw a distinct line between civilian life and the military while also maintaining militia forces of citizen soldiers. Militia members did not enjoy special status when they weren't on

Activists on both sides of the abortion issue protest in January 2013, the same week as the fortieth anniversary of the Supreme Court decision in *Roe v. Wade*, which legalized abortion.

active duty or conducting drills, and the Third Amendment protected ordinary citizens from abuses of power by militia members and regular soldiers. By drawing a sharp distinction between civilian and military life, they also wanted to protect the government from the possibility of being usurped by the military.

CONCLUSION

When it was written, the Third Amendment was ratified with very little debate and a high level of support. While there have not been any major instances of quartering for more than a century, troops have been deployed numerous times during natural disasters, such as in the aftermath of Hurricane Katrina. Without the amendment, the only protection citizens would have against military personnel coming into their homes is the self-restraint of the military itself, which could be severely stressed in the event of an emergency. Even if many Americans are unaware of the fact, this largely unremembered amendment continues to protect their rights in their own homes.

Tyron Garner (*left*) and John Lawrence (*right*) address supporters after winning their own case regarding the right to privacy.

THE BILL OF RIGHTS

First Amendment (proposed 1789; ratified 1791): Freedom of religion, speech, press, assembly, and petition

Second Amendment (proposed 1789; ratified 1791): Right to bear arms

Third Amendment (proposed 1789; ratified 1791): No quartering of soldiers in private houses in times of peace

Fourth Amendment (proposed 1789; ratified 1791): Interdiction of unreasonable search and seizure; requirement of search warrants

Fifth Amendment (proposed 1789; ratified 1791): Indictments; due process; self-incrimination; double jeopardy; eminent domain

Sixth Amendment (proposed 1789; ratified 1791): Right to a fair and speedy public trial; notice of accusations; confronting one's accuser; subpoenas; right to counsel

Seventh Amendment (proposed 1789; ratified 1791): Right to a trial by jury in civil cases

Eighth Amendment (proposed 1789; ratified 1791): No excessive bail and fines; no cruel or unusual punishment

Ninth Amendment (proposed 1789; ratified 1791): Protection of unenumerated rights (rights inferred from other legal rights but that are not themselves coded or enumerated in written constitution and laws)

Tenth Amendment (proposed 1789; ratified 1791): Limits the power of the federal government

Bibliography

ACLU.org. "Students: Your Right to Privacy." Retrieved December 2016. https://www.aclu.org/other/students-your-right-privacy.

Carey, Charles W., Jr., ed. *The American Revolution: Opposing Viewpoints*. Farmington Hills, MI: Greenhaven Press, 2005.

Chernow, Ron. *Alexander Hamilton*. New York, NY: Penguin Group, 2005.

Countryman, Edward. *The American Revolution*. New York, NY: Hill and Wang, 2003.

LambdaLegal.org. "Lawrence v. Texas." Retrieved December 2016. http://www.lambdalegal.org/in-court/cases/lawrence-v-texas.

Monk, Linda R. *The Words We Live By: Your Annotated Guide to the Constitution*. New York, NY: Stonesong Press, 2003.

Nash, Gary B. *The Unknown American Revolution*. New York, NY: Penguin Group, 2005.

Peltrason, J. W., and Sue Davis. *Understanding the Constitution*. Orlando, FL: Harcourt College Publishers, 2000.

PBS.org. "Griswold v. Connecticut (1965)." Retrieved December 2016. http://www.pbs.org/wnet/supremecourt/rights/landmark_griswold.html.

PBS.org. "Lawrence v. Texas (2003)." Retrieved December 2016. http://www.pbs.org/wnet/supremecourt/future/landmark_lawrence.html.

Rakove, Jack N. *Original Meanings: Politics and Ideas in the Making of the Constitution*. New York, NY: Vintage Books, 1996.

Roger, James P. "Third Amendment Protections in Domestic Disasters." *Cornell Journal of Law and Legal Practice*. Ithaca, NY: Cornell University Law School, 2008. Retrieved December 2016. http://www.lawschool.cornell.edu/research/JLPP/upload/Rogers.pdf.

USHistory.org. "Quartering Act of 1774." Philadelphia, PA: Independence Hall Association, 1995–2010. Retrieved December 2016. http://www.ushistory.org/DECLARATION/related/q74.html.

Vile, John R. A. *Companion to the United States Constitution and Its Amendments*. 4th ed. Westport, CT: Praeger Publishers, 2006.

Warren, Samuel D., and Brandeis, Louis D. *The Right to Privacy*. New Orleans, LA: Quid Pro Books, 2015.

Wood, Gordon S. "The Third Amendment." National Constitution Center. Retrieved December 2016. https://constitutioncenter.org/interactive-constitution/amendments/amendment-iii.

Glossary

ambassador A high-ranking official who represents the interests of one country to another.

assembly A body of elected political representatives, usually the lower house of a state legislature.

barracks A building or group of buildings used to house soldiers.

boycott To refuse to purchase products or services as a means of protest, or to apply pressure against an entity such as a nation, company, or organization.

convention A meeting or formal gathering of representatives or delegates to discuss and act on matters of common concern.

delegate A person chosen to act for or represent others.

garrison A place where troops are stationed.

indentured servant A person who came to America and was placed under contract to work for another person over a period of time.

insurrection An act or instance of rising up in revolt, rebellion, or resistance against a civil authority or an established government.

legislature A body of officials who have been elected or chosen to make, change, or repeal laws.

militia A body of citizens signed up for military service; militia members serve full-time only in emergencies.

petition A formally composed request, often containing the names of those making the request, that has been sent to people in power to ask for some favor, right, or other benefit.

quarter To house or give lodgings.

ratify To confirm by expressing approval or consent.

tyrannical Unjustly cruel, harsh, or severe.

Further Reading

BOOKS

Ellis, Carol. *The Military in Colonial America* (Life in Colonial America). New York, NY: Cavendish Square, 2014.

Kawa, Katie. *Bill of Rights* (Documents of American History). New York, NY: Rosen Publishing, 2017.

Keegan, Anna. *The United States Constitution and the Bill of Rights: The Law of the Land* (Spotlight on American History). New York, NY: Rosen Publishing, 2016.

Roxburgh, Ellis. *Alexander Hamilton vs. Aaron Burr: Duel to the Death* (History's Greatest Rivals). New York, NY: Gareth Stevens, 2015.

Shea, Therese. *The United States Constitution* (Documents That Shaped America). New York, NY: Gareth Stevens, 2014.

WEB SITES

Bill of Rights Institute
www.billofrightsinstitute.org

> The Bill of Rights Institute's mission is to educate young people about the words and ideas of America's founders, the liberties guaranteed in America's founding documents, and the continued impact of these principles.

Bostonian Society
www.bostonhistory.org

> The Bostonian Society is dedicated to studying and preserving Boston's history in the form of historic materials, records, and structures.

National Constitution Center
constitutioncenter.org

> The National Constitution Center is dedicated to promoting a better understanding of and appreciation for the US Constitution, its history, and its contemporary relevance.

Index